The
rock cake
assembly book

25 primary school assemblies

Tony Bower

**kevin
mayhew**

First published in 2005 by

KEVIN MAYHEW LTD
Buxhall, Stowmarket, Suffolk, IP14 3BW
E-mail: info@kevinmayhewltd.com

www.kevinmayhew.com

9 8 7 6 5 4 3 2 1 0

ISBN 1 84417 4387
Catalogue No. 1500803

Cover design by Angela Selfe
Edited and typeset by Graham Harris

Printed and bound in Great Britain

CONTENTS

PAGE

Introduction   5

IMAGINATIVE DRAMA STORIES

Would you believe it?   7

I doubt it   9

A fist full of fish   11

What a catch!   13

Someone you can count on   15

INTERACTIVE STORIES WITH ACTIONS

A helping hand   17

Seeing who can help   19

Ears to hear   21

Something to share   23

A sorry story   25

IMMEDIATE TWO-PERSON SKETCHES

The walk of faith   27

The parable of the unjust judge   29

The rich ruler   31

The parable of the lost sheep   33

Sower sketch   35

IMPROVISED DRAMAS

The parable of the two sons   37

Forgive what?   39

Anyone for a party?   41

What a waste   43

The whining workers   45

INSPIRATIONAL GROUP SKETCHES

Solid as a sandcastle   47

Some kind of friend   49

The light of understanding   51

Running the race   53

The parable of Pru   55

To Claire and Joseph, my primary people

A word of thanks to: Arkholme, Scotforth, Silverdale, St John's Ethel and Quernmore primary schools; and Debbie Green, without whom this book would not have been possible. Thank you.

Introduction

It's Monday morning and the bell's ringing. An alarm is also sounding in your head because it's assembly time and it's your turn to do it. Now what was that good idea you had over the weekend? And where did you put that piece of paper with the scribbled details? Even if that doesn't describe your approach to assemblies, there could be occasions when an assembly is required and time constraints have left you up against it and you're wondering what on earth to do. This book provides realistic, accessible material that has already been tried and tested in schools.

There are few props, there are no costumes (although you could choose to add some) and minimal preparation is required. Where children or other volunteers help with the drama, they can take their cue from you regarding actions. I've always found them very keen to build up their part in response to the narrator or characters speaking from the script (or ad-libbing, once the general gist of the dialogue has been absorbed). Either way, you should all have great fun – which is always one of the best ways to remember things.

Storytelling

Most of the assemblies fall into the category of telling a story. They are all interactive, with opportunities for the children to join in and take part. The story can be read from the page or memorised, paraphrased or adapted to suit you. Once you are familiar with the story, putting it in your own words or adapting to the children is essential, especially with improvised dramas. It's great doing stories with children being involved and responding to them. Even though the stories are here in black and white, whenever I have used them they invariably change – and benefit from being that flexible. So make them your own, while retaining the hooks. These remain the same – i.e. the rhymes or repetitions or the interactive parts.

It's like baking a batch of rock cakes. You mix the ingredients and put all the cakes in the oven. You create a nice batch of edible, home-baked cakes, but they are all slightly different shapes and sizes – and yet they are all recognisably rock cakes. You don't have any that have somehow transformed into jam tarts, for instance. It's the same with these assemblies. The ingredients will work if you apply them with a mix of fun and enjoyment. If you are happy telling the story or having fun doing some acting that will show and communicate volumes to the audience. If you enjoy working with children and can have fun with them, that will come across loud and clear. Nothing in these scripts or stories can provide those essential ingredients – only you can do that.

I have thoroughly enjoyed doing these assemblies and being a part of the school communities I work in. I do pray that you will enjoy performing them, too, and that you will have fun and leave behind a thought-provoking message.

Making connections

All the assemblies begin with asking the children a question or questions. You can add a personal story as well to introduce the subject. The questions may be simple and obvious but it begins to connect the child to the story you are about to do. In the closing part of the assembly you can finish by asking a few questions, helping the children to think through what's been presented or make a few comments and observations yourself – or even a mixture! Hopefully, whatever you do you will have stimulated the children in their thinking about faith and the way we live and why.

Suggested songs

At the end of each assembly outline there is a suggested song. Each song is available on the *No pianist for assembly? No problem!* set of CDs published by Kevin Mayhew, which features:

- High-quality accompaniments for 166 popular hymns and songs
- Separate disc of Christmas carols and songs
- Appropriate backing for each hymn featuring many different instruments and percussion
  Product code: 1490091
  Set of 8 CDs

This is complemented by the *Hymns and Songs for Assembly* words book.
  Product code: 1413191
  ISBN: 1 84003 929 9

Would you believe it?

Where in the Bible?
Luke 24:1-12

Way in | Hands up if you have ever tried to get someone to believe something you are saying, but they won't. How did you feel? How did you prove that what you were saying was true? I'm going to tell a story about some women in the Bible who had a story to tell – but their friends didn't believe it.

Setting the scene | In the story there will be a phrase that will be repeated. It goes like this: 'They closed their minds, they closed their ears, because they couldn't see what was meant to be.' (*Show simple actions, which go in four steps.*)

1 Hands on heads
2 Hands on ears
3 Hands on eyes
4 Hands held wide in an open gesture

(*Once the actions have been taught you can begin the story.*)

Story | They ran into the room, full of nervous energy, almost too excited to speak, jumping up and down like a fire cracker that had just been lit.

'He's not there,' cried Mary.

'He's risen,' shouted Joanna.

Their friends, the disciples, stared open-mouthed at the women who were wide-eyed and staring back at them.

'He's not there,' said Joanna.

'He's risen,' whispered Mary.

But the disciples didn't understand, so: **They closed their minds, they closed their ears because they couldn't see what was meant to be**.

The women were so excited they could hardly stand still. They tugged at the sleeves of their friends, wanting to take them to the tomb, wanting to show them it was true. They had seen with their own eyes, heard the voice of an angel speak to them, saying: 'Why do you look for the living among the dead? He is not here; he has risen! Remember how he told you, while he was still with you in Galilee? The Son of Man must be crucified but on the third day be raised again.'

But when they told the message to the disciples they said it was utter nonsense and: **They closed their minds, they closed their ears because they couldn't see what was meant to be**.

The women were desperate for them to believe. They knew that they were speaking the truth, no matter how unbelievable it sounded and seemed to the disciples.

But they couldn't understand, so: **They closed their minds, they**

closed their ears because they couldn't see what was meant to be.

How could they convince them? How could they make them believe? What would happen if they refused to leave the house? The women told the story. The tale of an empty tomb. The story of folded grave clothes. The tale of an angel. The story of the risen Jesus. It seemed like nonsense, it made no sense to the disciples. How could it be true? How could it possibly be true? But in the end there was only one thing to do.

Peter stood up and then he ran.

He ran out of the house and he ran down the road and he ran to the tomb and then he saw with his eyes and began to understand in his mind that what the women had said was true.

Jesus had risen.

Prayer Father God, we thank you for Easter and we thank you for Jesus. We thank you for an empty tomb and the women who believed that Jesus was alive again. Help us to tell the truth in our lives and please help us to listen to others. Amen.

Over to you Why do we sometimes find it hard to believe things? What do you think convinced the women in this story? Why do you think the men finally went to the tomb? How can we check out our faith?

Suggested songs *Give me joy in my heart*
Hosanna, Hosanna
I danced in the morning

I doubt it

Where in the Bible?
John 20:24-31

Way in | Hands up if you have ever heard something which you doubted but later found out was true. How did you feel when you were told the story? How did you feel when you found out it was true?

Sometimes things happen in life which sound unbelievable, but we later find out that they are true. There is a character in the Bible called Thomas, who was one of Jesus' disciples. He was a real friend and follower of Jesus, but he also found it hard sometimes to believe in things that Jesus said and did. This is what Thomas said after the resurrection of Jesus: 'Unless I see the nail marks in his hands and put my finger where the nails were, and put my hand into his side, I will not believe it.'

Setting the scene | We can now act this out together. For nails in his hands put your right finger into the palm of your left hand and then your left finger into the palm of your right hand. For side, put both your hands on one side of your body and then we all say together: '**I will not believe it**!'

Story | He paced around the room, hot and bothered, tired and confused.

'It's true Thomas.'

'Honest, Thomas, why would we lie to you?'

Thomas sat down and rubbed his forehead. He felt worn out with all the thinking he had been doing.

Jesus alive?

Jesus alive!

Thomas wanted to believe it, would love to have believed it, but there were facts that went against it. Things such as the fact that Jesus was dead. He had been killed, crucified. No, he couldn't believe it, he couldn't allow himself to believe it. It wasn't true, it just wasn't true.

He turned to his friends – his fellow disciples – and said (*actions*): '**Unless I see the nail marks in his hands and put my finger where the nails were, and put my hand into his side, I will not believe it**.'

Some of his friends shrugged their shoulders and some tried to persuade him, but nothing that anyone said could change his mind.

'**Unless I see the nail marks in his hands and put my finger where the nails were, and put my hand into his side, I will not believe it**.'

'So there,' thought Thomas. 'So there.'

He sat down on the floor, crossed his legs and stared at a beetle scuttling across the ground.

Under his breath you could hear him mutter: '**Unless I see the nail marks in his hands and put my finger where the nails were,**

and put my hand into his side I will not believe it.'

And he didn't believe it. He just couldn't believe it.

A week later the disciples were in the house again, and Thomas was with them. The doors were locked, sealed and bolted. Not even a mouse could get in the house.

'Peace be with you!'

Thomas almost fell on the floor.

He recognised that voice. He would know it anywhere.

He turned his head, his mind spinning.

Jesus.

Standing there, in the room, as large as life.

'Put your finger here; see my hands. Reach out your hand and put it into my side. Stop doubting and believe.'

Thomas just fell on the floor and said: 'My Lord and my God.'

Prayer Father God, thank you for Thomas. He's someone we can sympathise with and identify with. We sometimes struggle in our faith. We have doubts and find things difficult to believe. Please help us to find, like Thomas, the reality of your resurrection in our lives today. Amen.

Over to you Why do you think Thomas found it hard to believe? What convinced him of his faith? What proof do we have for our faith?

Suggested songs *God forgave my sin in Jesus' name*
How lovely on the mountains
Jesus' hands were kind hands

A fist full of fish

Where in the Bible?
Luke 5:1-11

Way in
Have you ever had a time when you couldn't do something and needed somebody's help? Here's something that happened to me. (*Give an example.*) How do you feel when you can't do it? How do you feel when you receive the help? We are going to look at a story in the Bible where someone was struggling until Jesus came along.

Setting the scene

> Row the boat, row the boat,
> throw out the net, throw out the net,
> haul in the fish, haul in the fish,
> what have we caught? . . . what have we caught? . . . Nothing!'

(*Put in a few simple actions to accompany the words.*)

Story
There once was a fisherman. He fished day and night, night and day. He was a hard working, boat rowing, net hauling, fish catching kinda guy.

One night he rowed out on to the lake to do some fishing. He had his nets ready – and his sandwiches, because it was going to be a long night. He had peanut butter, jam and marmalade sandwiches. Well maybe he didn't, but they do sound tasty, don't they? Maybe not!

The man saw the moon playing hide-and-seek, dodging behind the clouds floating in a starry sky. It was a beautiful, warm summer's evening to be out on the lake. Peter began to fish . . .

> **Row the boat, row the boat,**
> **throw out the net, throw out the net,**
> **haul in the fish, haul in the fish,**
> **what have we caught? . . . what have we caught? . . .**
> **Nothing!'**

Never mind. If at first you don't succeed, give in . . . (*pause*) No! Try again.

> **Row the boat, row the boat,**
> **throw out the net, throw out the net,**
> **haul in the fish, haul in the fish,**
> **what have we caught? . . . what have we caught? . . .**
> **Nothing!'**

Now the sun was coming up and rays of light were making the lake sparkle, but Peter didn't feel sparkling at all. He felt shattered, exhausted, worn out and full of deep, heavy sighs. With sagging shoulders and tired limbs he returned his boat to the shore. He thought that was the end of his night's work, but it wasn't.

A man called Jesus borrowed his boat to stand in and speak to the crowds. There were so many people lining the shore listening to Jesus that he had to find somewhere to stand so they could all hear . . . so he chose Peter's boat.

Peter listened and listened . . . and then he listened and listened some more. And he listened really carefully when Jesus said to him: 'Put out into deep water, and let down the nets for a catch.'

Peter answered: 'Master, we've worked hard day and night and haven't caught anything. But because you say so, I will let down the nets.'

So he let down the nets . . . and he waited . . . and he waited . . . and he waited, until he felt there was something pulling on the net, something heavy, something really heavy like a load of fish. So he hauled in the net and he looked inside and saw dozens and dozens of fish. And he looked at Jesus and fell on his knees.

Prayer Father God, thank you that you can help us when we cannot cope, when we are weak. Thank you that you are strong and able and willing to help us. Amen.

Over to you There is more to life than meets the eye. Jesus can do the miraculous and is willing to help us. How can we help others and offer our gifts and talents?

Suggested songs *Be bold, be strong*
Who's the king of the jungle?
Wide, wide as the ocean

What a catch!

Where in the Bible?
John 21:1-14

Way in (*Tell a story about forgiveness, maybe from your own life, but something that the children can relate to. Think of something you did that was silly or wrong and that you had to ask forgiveness for – or share an experience of when someone asked you to forgive them*). Have you ever done anything wrong and had to say sorry? (*You should have 100 per cent of the hands go up.*) How does it feel when you are forgiven? We are going to look at a story about someone who desperately needed forgiving.

Setting the scene (*Say the rhyme from the previous assembly, using the actions.*)
Row the boat, row the boat,
throw out the net, throw out the net,
haul in the fish, haul in the fish,
what have we caught? . . . what have we caught? . . .
Nothing!'

Story Peter was sad. He was really excited and thrilled that Jesus was alive again. That was amazing. It was a miracle and it was the best news ever, but there was still something not right. Peter had let Jesus down. On the night Jesus had been arrested Peter had been asked the question 'Do you know Jesus?' three times. The scene went a little bit like this. (*Encourage the children to ask the question all together, explaining that they will ask you three times, starting very quiet and getting louder and louder.*)
'Do you know Jesus?'
No.
'Do you know Jesus?'
No.
'Do you know Jesus?'
No.
Peter had let Jesus down. Imagine saying that you didn't know your best friend. Imagine saying it three times! So Peter felt bad – really, really, really bad. One night he decided to go out fishing with his friend, so he got in his boat and he would . . .
Row the boat, row the boat,
throw out the net, throw out the net,
haul in the fish, haul in the fish,
what have we caught? . . . what have we caught? . . . Nothing!'
Never mind. If at first you don't succeed give in . . . (*pause*) No! Try again.

> **Row the boat, row the boat,**
> **throw out the net, throw out the net,**
> **haul in the fish, haul in the fish,**
> **what have we caught? . . . what have we caught? . . . Nothing!'**

Now he felt tired – really, really tired. His arms ached, his back ached, his hands ached . . . his whole body ached.

The sun started to rise. Rays of light made the water shimmer in a golden glow. A figure appeared on the shore – a dark shape silhouetted in the early morning light.

'Friends, haven't you any fish?' the stranger on the shore called out.

'No,' came the shouted response from the fishermen.

'Throw your net on the right side of the boat and you will find some.'

Peter picked up the net, tired and weary, his eyes bleary – and threw the net over the boat and waited . . . and waited . . . and waited . . . and . . . wait a minute, wait a minute, what is this? What's going on? Peter was pulling the net but the net was pulling him. He struggled and he strived to catch those fish alive.

Then Peter's friend shouted: 'It's the Lord' and that was enough for Peter. He jumped out of the boat, he waded through the water and he ran on to the shore. There was the smell of cooked breakfast. A barbecue on the beach. Jesus the chef had prepared a meal for them all to eat. It smelled delicious and it tasted delicious.

After breakfast Jesus went for a walk with Peter. He wanted to talk to him. Jesus asked Peter a question and this is what he asked:

(*Encourage the children to say the line: 'Do you love me?' three times.*)

'Do you love me?
Yes.
'Do you love me?'
Yes.
'Do you love me?'
Yes.

Then Jesus said: 'Feed my sheep, take care of my lambs.' And he wasn't talking about the sheep in the field, but people. He was giving Peter a massive job to do and showing him that he really was forgiven and that he was a friend whom Jesus loved and trusted.

Prayer | Father God, thank you that you do love us and you do forgive us when we are sorry for the things we've done wrong. Please help us to be like you and forgive others too. Amen.

Over to you | Talk about how important it is to forgive someone when they are sorry. How would we feel if people didn't forgive us? What would the consequences be if people didn't forgive?

Suggested songs | *I'm accepted, I'm forgiven*
I'm special
Abba, Father

Someone you can count on

Where in the Bible?
Luke 5:27-32

Way in | (*Tell a story of when you needed someone's help.*) Can you think of things that you need help with? We all need help from time to time in lots of different ways. We are going to look at a story from the Bible about a person called Levi, who needed Jesus' help.

Setting the scene | (*Teach the children the following rhyme, using appropriate actions to demonstrate what you are saying.*)
> One for you, one for me,
> one for you, two for me,
> one for you, time for tea . . . slurp!

Story | There was a man in the Bible called Levi. He was very good at counting and used his fingers to do so. Let's try and count as fast as him. (*Using your fingers, count from one to 10, then ask the children to join in, getting faster and faster, making it into a race to see if they can keep up with you.*)

Levi could count and count. He loved to count all day. He sat at his tax booth collecting taxes from the people. But this is how he used to count.
> **One for you, one for me,**
> **one for you, two for me,**
> **one for you, time for tea . . . slurp!**

Levi was cheating people out of their hard-earned income and taking money that just didn't belong to him. It was a case of . . .
> **One for you, one for me,**
> **one for you, two for me,**
> **one for you, time for tea . . . slurp!**

Levi would do this all day long, and you could count on him to do this forever and ever because he loved counting and nothing was going to change. Yet something needed to change.

Just imagine what your clothes would be like if you wore them every single day! Day after day after day after day. What would they be like? It would cause a real stink. Other people would smell it and it wouldn't be very nice at all. Not for you and not for anyone else.

Well, sometimes there are things on the inside that need changing, too. Things like cheating and lying and being mean. We need to change this bad behaviour or it will make a mess of our lives and upset other people, too. That's what Levi needed to do . . . but how could he do it? How could he possibly change? Who could he count on to help him?

One day a man passed by his tax booth and said to Levi: 'Follow me.'

Why should Levi follow him? Could he count on him to help him change?

The man who said 'Follow me' was Jesus.

Levi not only decided there and then that he was going to follow Jesus but he was also going to throw a big party for him and invite all his friends, so they could meet Jesus.

At the party all Levi's friends were having a great time.

Here's what we'll do. Half of you can be party guests and say: 'Munch, munch, slurp slurp.' (*Show the children a couple of simple actions to copy, and rehearse it once or twice.*)

But there were other people there who were not friends of Levi or friends of Jesus. They were the Pharisees and teachers of the law and they couldn't see how someone like Levi could possibly change. They didn't count on Jesus being able to change people, so they just grumbled.

Here's what the other half of you can say: 'Mumble, mumble, grumble, grumble, ge-r-r-r-r-r!' and give a nice big scowl at the end! (*Rehearse this a couple of times through.*)

OK here we go at the party. There was Levi and his friends having a great time . . . (*Point to the first group to say their lines.*)

. . . but then the Pharisees and teachers of the law complained . . . (*Point to the other group.*)

. . . and this kept going on and on and on. (*Point to both groups at the same time and keep repeating until you want to stop!*)

Jesus told the Pharisees: 'It's not the healthy who needed a doctor, but the sick.'

Levi was someone who had needed the love and help of Jesus to change and to get better and become a better person. He became a follower of Jesus. He still loved counting and he knew he could count on Jesus.

(*Hold up your fingers one by one as you say the next lines. There are ten words.*)

I can count on Jesus. His love will never change.

(*Invite the children to copy and repeat a good few times.*)

Prayer Father God, thank you that you do love us and can help us to change and be more like you. Amen.

Over to you It is possible for people to change. We all do things wrong and putting a stop to it is very important. Sometimes we might need other people's help to change our ways.

Suggested songs *I'm accepted, I'm forgiven*
Make me a channel of your peace
Lord of all hopefulness

A helping hand

Where in the Bible?
Luke 10:25-37

Way in What kind of people help us in life? (*Talk about how we need the emergency services and what would happen if we didn't have those people to help us.*)

Setting the scene Jesus said that we should love our neighbour, so somebody asked him: 'Who is my neighbour?'

We probably all have neighbours. People who live next door to us. Is that what Jesus meant? To show what he did mean about loving our neighbour Jesus told a story.

In our story I am going to be using my hands to show what is happening and acting out some of the dramatic moments, just by using my hands. You can join in the acting, too, by copying my 'hand' actions.

Story This is the story all about a man who one day decided to go on a journey, so he packed his bags (*act out packing a bag*), waved goodbye to his family (*wave*) and patted the dog, which licked his hand, ugh!

This story is from a long time ago, before the invention of cars, trains and planes, so the man had to ride on a donkey. He fed the donkey a nice juicy carrot before they set off (*mime this action*). The donkey loved carrots and gobbled it all up and would have nibbled the man's hands if he hadn't quickly pulled them out of the way. Now that the donkey was fed and the man's bags were packed everything was ready for his journey. The man took hold of the donkey's reins and they set off.

The journey was from Jerusalem to Jericho. As they travelled in the heat of the day the man grew very tired (*stifle a yawn*) and very hot (*wipe your forehead*). The sun's rays made the road shimmer in the dazzling heat. Maybe it was because of the bright light or the tiredness, but for whatever reason, the man didn't see the robbers attack. A-a-r-g-h! (*Both hands go up in front of your face.*)

He held up his hands to try to defend himself but it was no good, the robbers were too strong and there were too many. They beat him up (*mime blows*), took all his money (*act out stealing*), and went away pulling faces at the man on the ground (*put your thumb on the end of your nose*). They left the man with nothing but bruises.

Lying on the floor the man heard a noise. It was the sound of footsteps. Someone was passing.

It was a priest.

The man held up his hand, hoping the priest would take it and help him up. The priest saw the man and his hand and saw that he had been beaten up. He wasn't going to get involved, so he just folded his arms and carried on. Oh dear . . . whatever is going to happen to the poor fellow on the floor? He can't take any more of the heat and the hurt of the sun and his sores.

He thought he heard more footsteps, so he put his hand to his ear and the sounds he heard confirmed it. There was someone else passing by. He quickly held out his hand and hoped the person would be kind enough to help.

The man on the road was a very religious man, a well-respected man, but not a man who was going to get his hands dirty. No! He liked to keep them nice and clean, so he washed his hands of the whole situation (*mime washing hands*) and passed on by.

Now the man on the ground thought that he'd had it. He had no money, no friends to help him, and the day was getting hotter and hotter. He put his hands over his face to try to protect it from the scorching sun. He knew that he needed water and he needed it very soon.

There were more footsteps and the sound of a voice. It was an accent he recognised – the voice of a Samaritan man, the enemies of his people. There was more chance of winning the lottery – and they didn't have a lottery in those days – than of this man helping him out. Or so he thought.

The Samaritan didn't ignore what he'd seen or shield his eyes from reality, but he actually became involved. He bandaged the man's wounds, gave him water to drink, helped him up on to his feet, let him ride on his donkey and took him to an inn, where he paid silver coins for him to stay and be looked after.

The man who had been robbed was amazed, and didn't know what to say, but he shook the man's hands – the man whom he thought was an enemy but turned out to be a friend.

In our lives what will we do with our hands? Will we use them to make fun of people (*pull a face*), hurt people (*smack one fist into the palm of the other hand*) or ignore people (*turn your back*) or choose to not help (*sneer*). Or will we reach out our hands to help? Will we be friends like the Samaritan man?

Prayer Father God, thank you that you teach us that everyone matters to you and everyone is our neighbour. Please help us to be helpful neighbours to one another today. Amen.

Over to you Ask the children again who they think their neighbour is and see what they say. Think about the ways in which we can help others.

Suggested songs *When I needed a neighbour*
I, the Lord of sea and sky
I will bring to you the best I can

Seeing who can help

Where in the Bible?
Mark 10:46-52

Way in Can you name the type of people who help us? Here are some suggestions. Who helps when we are stuck on a really difficult maths question? Who helps when we need to cross the road safely? Sometimes we have a choice as to who can help, but hopefully we all have someone we can turn to for help.

Setting the scene We're going to be looking at a character in the Bible called Bartimaeus. He needed help, and we'll see that he knew who to turn to, even though he couldn't see.

Story Day after day, sitting by the roadside, Bartimaeus begged for food. It wasn't a lot of fun begging for food. Can you imagine what it might have been like? Let's try and see if we can.

Hold out your hands, now close your eyes and on the count of three say: 'Please can I have some food?'

Sometimes his hands were filled with good things to eat, sometimes scraps or crumbs, but most often it was filled with nothing. He had empty hands that waited . . . and waited . . . and waited.

One day a large crowd gathered by the roadside. Bartimaeus could hear them talking. He could hear the excitement in the crowd but he couldn't tell what was going on. However, he knew that the hubbub was about somebody very special who was coming along. He tried to listen really hard. He could hear a donkey snorting, so he listened again. This time he heard a horse's hooves . . . then a buzzing insect, which he tried to swat away. He kept listening . . . and listening . . . and listening . . . and listening.

The crowd began to get very excited, and he could hear them murmuring and muttering. Like ripples on a pond the word spread throughout the crowd. (*Starting at one side of the hall encourage the children to quietly say the name 'Jesus', and then signal to others to join in gradually, until the whole assembly is saying Jesus' name.*)

The word on the street – the word running through the crowd – was Jesus. Jesus was coming. The teacher, the preacher, the healer was on his way.

As soon as Bartimaeus heard who was coming he started to shout.

(*Ask one half of the assembly to shout 'Jesus, have mercy' and the other half to say 'Sssh' – keep repeating.*)

Jesus suddenly stopped. The crowd held their breath. Bartimaeus clung onto his hope.

'Call him,' said Jesus. So they called to Bartimaeus: 'Cheer up, get on your feet. He's calling you.'

Throwing his cloak aside, Bartimaeus jumped to his feet and came running to Jesus.

He stood before Jesus, not able to see him but understanding that Jesus was the one who could help him.

'What do you want me to do for you?' Jesus asked him.

'Teacher, I want to see.'

The crowd held their breath and Bartimaeus received his sight.

'Go,' said Jesus. 'Your faith has healed you.'

And Bartimaeus went. He went down the road, following Jesus.

Prayer Father God, thank you for all the people who help us. Please help us to see what we can do for others. Amen.

Over to you Think about ways in which we can help other people. How can we make sure that our eyes are open to the need of others?

Suggested songs *This little light of mine*
Lord, the light of your love
God is love, his the care

Ears to hear

Where in the Bible?
Luke 10:38-42

Way in Are you good listeners? When do you think you might not be very good at listening? What distracts us or stops us from listening? Why is listening so important?

Setting the scene This story is about two sisters who were very different. One of them was a really good listener and the other one . . . well, you'll have to listen to the story to find out.

Story Once there were two sisters, whose names both started with the letter M. M for Mary and M for Martha. Martha would always say things like: 'Mmm . . . there's a job I need to do,' while Mary would say: 'Mmm . . . I'll have to think about that.'

(*Split the assembly in half and encourage one group to say the Martha lines and the other group Mary's words.*)

Whenever Martha saw some mess in the house she would say . . . (*wait for the children to say their line*) and whenever Mary faced a problem she would say . . . (*wait for the other group to say their line*).

The two sisters were very different, but they both had the same friend – Jesus.

One day there was a knock at the door. Mary thought about opening it but Martha was the one who got up and let Jesus into the house. Jesus is in the house! Jesus is in the house! Jesus is in the house! Martha could hardly stand still – she hopped on one foot and she hopped on the other and then she hopped around in a circle. She was hopping mad that Mary wasn't doing anything to help her with all the work that needed to be done. Martha decided she would have to do everything on her own.

(*Encourage the group who are Martha to copy your actions for her.*)

Martha rolled up her sleeves, picked up her duster and . . .

> She dusted up high,
> she dusted down low.
> Here some dust,
> there some dust,
> everywhere a bit of dust dust.
> (*Repeat*)

. . . and when she looked at Mary she simply saw her sitting at the feet of Jesus, listening . . .

> Mary listened carefully,
> to what Jesus had to tell.
> Mary's face just said it all,
> she listened really well.
>
> (*Repeat*)

21

Meanwhile, Martha was racing around the house like some cartoon character. Her legs were whizzing, her arms were flapping and her head was spinning. But Mary was sitting, listening, thinking . . . sitting, listening, thinking.

(*Repeat with both groups getting louder and louder.*)

Eventually, Martha couldn't take it any more. She turned to Jesus and said: 'Lord, don't you care that my sister has left me to do the work by myself? Tell her to help me!'

Jesus answered: 'Martha, Martha. You are worried and upset about many things, but only one thing is needed. Mary has chosen what is better and it will not be taken from her.'

Prayer Father God, thank you for giving us ears to hear, please help us to use them. Amen.

Over to you How can we make sure that we are good listeners? Why is listening so important? What sort of things might happen if we don't listen?

Suggested songs *Seek ye first the kingdom of God*
Be still and know that I am God
Colours of day

Something to share

Where in the Bible?
Luke 9:10-17

Way in We're going to think about sharing. Are you good at sharing? Hands up for 'yes' . . . Now, hands up for 'no' . . . and hands up for 'sometimes'.

Setting the scene We are going to be looking at a story in the Bible all about a young boy. To do this story you will all need to follow my hand actions and copy them as we go.

Story This is a story all about a young man who went on a picnic. He put in his lunch box 1, 2, 3, 4, 5 loaves of bread (*use your fingers to count this out*) and two delicious fish (*act this out with your hands*). He was so excited about where he was going he couldn't wait to leave the house. He grabbed hold of the door but his mum grabbed hold of him.

'You are not going anywhere until I have checked that you are nice and clean,' she said. 'Hold out your hands.'

So he held out his hands.

'Turn them over.'

So he turned them over.

'They need a good wash, my lad.'

So he gave them a good wash and raced to the door, but before he could go any further his mum had grabbed him again.

'I haven't checked behind your ears yet, laddie boy.'

So she checked behind his ears.

'I could grow some spuds in those ears. They're filthy.'

So she gave them a really good wash.

'Right, now you can go.' And as he left the house he waved goodbye to his mum.

The boy was very excited because he was going to see a man called Jesus. He had heard a lot about him and couldn't wait to listen to him. When he arrived it was already late in the morning and there was already a large crowd. The boy shielded his eyes from the sun and tried to see how many people were there. He thought he might be able to count so he began 1, 2, 3, 4, 5 (*get faster and faster and faster using your fingers, your toes and even your nose*). There were thousands and thousands of people there. It was the biggest crowd he had ever seen. Now the boy was even more excited and he sat down to listen.

Morning turned into afternoon, and he soon needed to eat, because his tummy was beginning to rumble. Every time it made a funny noise he put his hand there to try and stop it and make it be quiet, but it was getting louder and louder. It wasn't just his tummy, either – there were loads of people around him whose tummies were making very loud noises. People were getting very hungry. He couldn't wait to eat his lunch. He opened his lunch box and counted again . . . 1, 2, 3, 4, 5 barley loaves and 1, 2 little fish. He licked his lips and rubbed his tummy.

'Excuse me, but do you have any food?' said a voice.

The boy looked up, squinting in the sun. It was one of the disciples of Jesus speaking and he was asking if anyone had brought food to eat. The crowd kept saying 'No.'

'No, no, no.' And then more people said: 'No, no, no,' and still others said: 'No, no, no.'

No one had brought anything to eat but him. What was he going to do? He scratched his head and tried to think. He was very hungry, and so was everyone else, but no matter how much he thought, he couldn't understand what was going to happen. How could his food feed more than a few? He just didn't know what to do.

Thumbs up if you think he should give up his food or thumbs down if you think he should eat it himself.

Well, this is what the little boy did. He held out his food and gave it to the disciple of Jesus, who gave it to Jesus, who took it and broke the bread and gave it back to the disciples to give out. And they gave some, and gave some and gave some – and they gave some more until everyone had had some and there was some left over. There was so much left over that he went home with more food in his lunch box than when he started. More than the 1, 2, 3, 4, 5 barley loaves and 1, 2 fish, but he'd learned that giving and sharing is better than being selfish and keeping things to yourself.

Prayer Father God, thank you for people who share with us. Please help us to share what we have with others. Amen.

Over to you It doesn't matter if we think we have only a little to give – it's our attitude that counts. We may never see how far our giving goes or where our acts of kindness will lead, but we can trust that they will go further than we can possibly imagine.

Suggested songs *Father, I place into your hands*
This little light of mine
All over the world

A sorry story

Where in the Bible?
Luke 18:9-14

Way in What do we need to say when we've done something wrong? What is the magic word, as mums and dads sometimes call it? Why is it important to say sorry?

Setting the scene We are going to be thinking about a story that Jesus told concerning two people. One of them was a very proud man – a Pharisee – and the other was a very sorry man – a tax collector.

Story (*Divide the assembly in half and make half of the group the Pharisee and the other half the tax collector. Ask them all to stand up.*)

One fine morning two men decided to go to the temple and pray. One of them was a very proud, puffed up, full-of-himself Pharisee who marched with a swagger and held his head high and stuck his chin out. (*Ask the children to mime this, marching on the spot.*)

The other man was a tax collector, who had cheated people and robbed people of their hard-earned income. He walked slowly, shuffling his feet on the floor, with his head down and his bottom lip sticking out because he was feeling very sad. (*Again, ask the children to copy those actions, again without moving from the spot.*)

When they reached the temple the Pharisee held his hands up high and reached to heaven with his big head and said: 'God, I thank you that I am not like other men' and then he looked at the tax collector and tutted. (*Get the Pharisee children to do this.*)

'I am not a robber or an evildoer or a tax collector. I fast twice a week and give a tenth of all I get.'

Then he smiled a big cheesy smile and said 'Yes!' (*Again, ask them to follow the action.*)

The tax collector, on the other hand, would not even look up to heaven. He knelt down on the floor and whispered: 'God, have mercy on me, a sinner.' (*Ask the tax collector children to do those actions.*)

Jesus said: 'I tell you the truth. This man, this tax collector, went home from the temple right before God because he was sorry in his heart for all the wrong he'd done, but not the Pharisee – who was full of pride and couldn't see just how bad he was on the inside.'

Prayer Father God, thank you that you do forgive us when we say we are sorry and truly mean it. Amen.

Over to you When we do things we know are wrong it is important that we say sorry. What would happen if we didn't say sorry? What would we be like if we thought we were always brilliant and better than other people, like the Pharisee did? Would we be the kind of person that people would like to be friends with, or not? What kind of person should we be?

Suggested songs | *Abba, Father*
Father, we adore you
God forgave my sin in Jesus' name

The walk of faith

Where in the Bible?
Mattew 14:22-33

Way in	Who likes the dark? Is anyone scared of being in the dark? Sometimes we don't like the dark because we can't see where we're going or our imagination runs away with strange ideas.
Setting the scene	We're going to look at a story from the Bible about one of the disciples – Peter – who was scared of what he saw in the dark.
Characters	Narrator, Peter
Narrator	Imagine a dark night. No stars are shining and the moon is hiding behind the clouds. Some fishermen are sleeping on a boat. They might have sounded a little bit like this . . .
Peter	(*Loud snores, getting louder and louder.*)
Narrator	The fishermen were tired. That's why they were sound asleep and making all kinds of weird sounds like this . . .
P	(*Make very funny snoring sounds.*)
N	They had enjoyed another amazing day with Jesus. They had seen Jesus perform a miracle, feeding about 5000 people with only a few fish and five loaves of bread. Maybe while they were asleep they were dreaming about the day.
P	(*Without opening his eyes.*) While I'm asleep I'm dreaming about the day.
N	He was dreaming about the fish . . .
P	I'm dreaming about the fish.
N	He was dreaming about the bread . . .
P	I'm dreaming about the bread.
N	And he was dreaming about all the people who were fed . . .
P	I'm dreaming about all the people who were fed.
N	But then the wind began to blow (*ask the children to make gentle blowing sounds*) and the boat began to rock.
P	(*Peter starts to sway from side to side.*)
N	And the wind blew harder and harder. (*Encourage the children to follow your direction.*)
P	(*Peter rocks more vigorously from side to side.*)
N	And as the wind was blowing so hard against the boat, Peter woke up.
P	I'm awake now. Look at the waves. They're really making the boat go up and down, up and down, up and down. If I weren't such an experienced fisherman I'd be feeling sea-sick by now, (*goes to act out being sick*) but I am an experienced fisherman so I'm OK.
N	Meanwhile, on the mountainside, Jesus had been praying, but now it was time for him to go and join the disciples. They were out on the lake and he didn't have a boat, but he did have his legs and he

could walk, so that's what he did. He started to walk. He walked down the mountain, down the hill, along the path and he kept on going. He walked on to the shore and then kept going even further, out on to the lake – Jesus could take command over nature because he was the creator.

P Ooh, I must be going funny in the head, because I think I can see someone . . . on the water. (*Suddenly does a double take when he says this.*) On the water! (*He rubs his eyes and looks again.*) Th . . . th . . . this c-c-can't be right. It looks like a ghost! Whatever it is, it's giving me an awful fright.

N Peter was so scared you could hear his knees knocking . . .

P Knock! Knock! Knock!

N Peter was so scared you could hear his teeth chattering . . .

P Chatter, chatter, chatter! Chatter, chatter, chatter! Chatter, chatter, chatter!

N Peter was so scared he felt like crying . . .

P Aargh! Aargh! Aargh!

N Peter thought it was a ghost . . .

P I think it's a ghost.

N Jesus heard him and shouted: 'Take courage! It is I. Don't be afraid.'

P Lord, if it's you, tell me to come to you on the water.

N 'Come,' said Jesus, and Peter got out of the boat.

P I'm doing it, I'm doing it, I'm walking on the water, I'm walking on the water.

N And Peter was doing fine whenever he looked straight ahead at Jesus, but when the wind blew . . .

P (*Peter sways.*)

N Peter was afraid and started to sink.

P (*Peter starts to sink down.*) Lord, save me!

N Jesus reached out his hand and said: 'You of little faith. Why did you doubt?' Peter climbed back into the boat and fell on his knees and said . . .

P Truly, you are the Son of God.

N And the wind died down.

Prayer Father God, thank you that we can trust in you and you never let us down. Even when we feel like we are sinking you are always there. Amen.

Over to you Faith can be a mystery. We don't always see God with our eyes or understand with our minds, but we can still trust him. Talk about what faith really means. How we can trust in God even though we can't see him; that God is able to do things that we can't because he is God, just as Jesus – God's Son – could walk on water. We can't do that but we can put our trust in the God over all of creation.

Suggested songs *Be bold, be strong*
Be still, for the presence of the Lord
Father, I place into your hands

The parable of the unjust judge

Where in the Bible?
Luke 18:1-8

Way in	Are you good at keeping on going with things or do you give in easily? (*Share a story from your life to illustrate this. I told the tale of how I failed my driving test twice but was encouraged to keep on going and finally passed at the third attempt.*)
Setting the scene	Today we are going to look at a story that Jesus told about someone who didn't give up.
Characters	Narrator, Man
Narrator	This is the story all about a man . . .
Man	Hello, I'm a man.
N	Who was a grumpy man . . .
M	I'm a grumpy man.
N	He loved saying the word . . .
M	No.
N	If his children wanted some sweets . . .
M	No.
N	If his friends wanted some help . . .
M	No.
N	If a poor old widow needed his help . . .
M	No.
N	This man was a judge, but you can judge for yourselves if you think he is going to help the little old widow.
M	I'm not going to help her, I'm not. I'm too busy to help her. I'm too busy sitting in my garden watching the grass grow. It takes a lot of watching does the grass because it grows very, very slowly.
N	But the widow wouldn't give up. She would go to his house and (*raise your voice*) shout through the letterbox. She would phone him . . . ring ring, ring ring.
M	Hello, who is it? Oh no, it's you again.
N	And he would slam down the phone.
M	Slam!
N	So she would e-mail him, send him letters, camp out in his office and day and night she wouldn't give in, asking for justice. This is what she would say to the judge: 'Grant me justice.' (*Teach the children to say the words, getting louder and louder.*)
M	I'm not going to listen, I'm not going to hear, I know . . . I'll stick my fingers in my ears. (*He sticks his fingers in his ears while the children are shouting and getting louder.*)
M	Oh, OK, even though I don't care about God or anyone else I'll still do it, because she's not given up day or night. Justice will be served.

N | Jesus said: 'Will not God bring about justice to his chosen ones who cry out day and night?'

Prayer | Father God, thank you that you do hear our prayers. Please help us to do what's right and not to give up or give in. Amen.

Over to you | Sometimes in life we have to keep on trying and not give up. It's not always easy – it's often hard – but think about the benefits if we persevere.

Suggested songs | *This little light of mine*
This is the day
I, the Lord of sea and sky

The rich ruler

Where in the Bible?
Luke 18:18-29

Way in | Who has ever done a jigsaw puzzle? Who has ever tried to do a puzzle and found that you have pieces missing? It can be very frustrating! If you have only 999 pieces of a 1,000-piece jigsaw, even with only one piece missing, it still means that the picture is incomplete.

Setting the scene | Today we are going to look at a story from the gospels about a man who on the face of it had everything – but there was a vital piece of the jigsaw missing.

Characters | Narrator, Man

Narrator | This is the story about someone who had bags and bags and bags . . .

Man | (*On rushes a man carrying lots of shopping bags. He waves them about happily.*)

N | . . . of money, not shopping bags!

M | (*The man looks sheepish and throws the bags away*)

N | He had plenty of cash in his pockets . . .

M | (*The man pats his pockets*)

N | . . . he had plenty of coins to jingle . . .

M | (*The man looks in his pockets. He doesn't have any coins. He looks around desperately. He doesn't know what to do. Suddenly he has a bright idea.*) Jingle-jingle. Jingle-jingle. (*He says this and pretends he has coins in his hands to jingle.*)

N | The man had everything that money could buy . . .

M | I have everything that money can buy.

N | But he still felt something was missing . . .

M | I still feel that something is missing.

N | He was a rich young ruler . . .

M | (*The man looks at him clueless.*)

N | He was a rich young ruler . . .

M | (*The man dashes off and comes back on carrying a ruler.*)

N | . . . who ruled over people . . .

M | (*He holds the ruler out over the audience.*)

N | Not that kind of ruler!

M | (*He puts the ruler down.*)

N | He had money, power and position but there was still something missing . . .

M | I have money, power and position but there's still something missing.

N | He looked high . . .

M | (*The man acts out looking high.*)

N | . . . he looked low . . .

M	(*The man acts out looking low.*)
N	Until there was nowhere left to go.
M	(*The man looks all around but doesn't know where to go.*)
N	Until he heard about a man called Jesus.
M	(*He cups his hand to his ear.*)
N	He'd heard that Jesus was a teacher, a preacher of God's word. He went to see him and showed him great respect.
M	(*The man kneels on the ground.*)
N	What was it that was missing from his life? He had brains ...
M	(*Taps his head.*)
N	... he had money ...
M	(*Taps his pocket.*)
N	... but there was something missing on the inside ... (*The man stands up and touches his heart.*)
M/N	Eternal life!
Prayer	Father God, thank you for life and the promise through Jesus of eternal life. Thank you that it is a gift we can receive, for now and for ever. Amen.
Over to you	What do you think might have happened next? Why might the man have walked away? What would he have been missing if he did ignore Jesus?
Suggested songs	*Abba, Father* *Father God, I wonder* *Give me joy in my heart*

The parable of the lost sheep

Where in the Bible?
Luke 15:1-7

Way in	How many people here have any animals? Have those animals ever escaped or got lost? How did you feel when you realised they were missing?
Setting the scene	We are going to look at a parable of Jesus to do with missing animals.
Characters	Narrator, Sheep
Narrator	This morning I want to tell you a story . . .
Sheep	Can I help, can I help?
N	Well, I don't know.
S	Please, I'll be very good.
N	Well . . . OK then, but you must do what I say, all right?
S	OK.
N	This is the story of a sheep.
S	Moo! Moo!
N	That was a very good . . . cow, but I said sheep! Try again, please. This is the story of a sheep.
S	Meow! Meow!
N	That was a very good . . . cat! I said sheep!
S	Ooops, sorry.
N	This is the story of a sheep.
S	Baah! Baah!
N	One day, the sheep wandered away from the rest of the flock. (*Narrator indicates for the sheep to wander away.*) The sheep went so far away that it couldn't find its way back home. It was lost.
S	Oh no, I'm lost.
N	A-a-h!
S	And I'm lonely.
N	A-a-a-h!
S	And I'm scared.
N	A-a-a-a-h!
S	I want my mummy!
N	The shepherd, realising one of his sheep was missing, set off to find it. (*The two walk in opposite directions.*)
N	Children, if you see my sheep will you point and tell me, please? (*The children will usually shout and point enthusiastically! Keep on crossing over until you decide it is time to find your sheep.*)
N	Now, if everyone is quiet I am sure I could hear my lost sheep.
S	Mummy, mummy, mummy.

N | That sounds like my lost sheep.
(They walk slowly towards one another, back to back until they walk into each other.)
S | Mummy!
N | Well I'm really glad I found you.
S | So am I . . . that was a nice story.

Prayer | Father God, thank you that you care about all of us. Every single person here is special and precious to you, thank you. Amen.

Over to you | Why do you think the shepherd went to look for the missing sheep? What does that teach us about God?

Suggested songs | *If I were a butterfly*
Lord of all hopefulness
He's got the whole world in his hand

Sower sketch

Where in the Bible?
Matthew 13:1-8

Way in	How do crops grow? What do they grow from?
Setting the scene	We are going to look at a parable that Jesus taught, and it's all to do with crops and seeds.
Characters	Narrator, Men
Narrator	This is the story about a man . . .
Man	(*Man turns around. He is very energetic! Narrator coughs.*)
N	A quiet man.
M	Sorry.
N	Let's start again. This is the story all about a man.
M	(*Man turns round.*) Hello, I'm a quiet man.
N	Who one day decided to go into the field to sow some seed.
M	I've just decided to go into the field to sow some seed. (*Singing.*) We plough the field and scatter the good seed on the path. Yeah, the path . . . so the birds can come down and have a really nice picnic!
N	That is what the birds would do.
M	I know.
N	And then there would be no crops because the birds would have eaten it all up!
M	Ooops!
N	You'd better try again.
M	I'd better try again. I know! I'll put the seed among all the big rocks. Now watch them grow.
N	Oh dear, oh dear, oh dear.
M	Oh dear?
N	Look at what's happening to the crops.
M	They're growing.
N	I know they're growing . . . but look at their roots.
M	What roots?
N	They have no roots.
M	Oh no, no roots means . . .
N/M	They're going to die.
N	Time to try again.
M	I'd better try again. I know! I can put them near these other plants.
N	They're weeds.
M	They're only little weeds. Look at the seed grow. Wow!
N	Now watch what happens to the seeds.
M	(*Man acts out watching.*) I can't see what's happening.
N	Keep looking.
M	I can't see anything.

N Keep looking. (*While the narrator is talking they are creeping up on the man with their hands outstretched to throttle him!*)

M Aaarrghh! That's not healthy.

N (*The narrator lets go*) No it's not! You'd better try again or you'll *land* yourself in more trouble.

M I have no idea what to do. I will land myself in trouble.

N (*The narrator coughs.*)

M Have you got a bad cough?

N Land, land, *land*.

M (*Slowly dawning on him.*) Land! *Land!* (*He throws the seeds high in the air and watches them all land.*)

N Now, because they fell in fertile soil, look at them grow with the sun and the rain.

M (*He acts out watching them grow really tall.*) Wow!

Prayer Father God, thank you that you want us to grow to be like you. Please help us to listen to you and put your words into practice. Amen.

Over to you Why did the plants only grow in the good soil? What does it mean for us to be like that good soil?

Suggested songs *Make me a channel of your peace*
I will bring to you
Colours of day

The parable of the two sons

Where in the Bible?
Matthew 21:28-32

Way in | Who is good at volunteering to do jobs – at school, at home and anywhere else a job needs to be done? Tell me what sort of jobs you volunteer for.

Setting the scene | We're going to hear a parable that Jesus taught about two sons who needed to get a job done.
(*Ask for two volunteers, and then you can begin.*)

Story | This is the story of a man who had two sons – one called Bill and the other called Ben. They loved playing in the garden and they especially loved playing with weeds. You could even say that they were potty about the garden. One day, Dad asked Bill if he would help to do some digging. Bill pulled a face (*invite the actor to make a face*) and said: 'I will not.' (*Ask him to repeat the words and say them with attitude.*) He stamped his feet (*ask him to act out these actions*), he shook his head and said: 'No, no. no.'

'Oh dear, oh dear, oh dear,' thought Dad, as his son stomped away and sat down. The father turned to his second son and asked him the same question: 'Will you work in our garden today?'

The second son jumped for joy (*ask him to do the actions*). He was so excited that he jumped even higher, because he had so much joy! He was so excited and thrilled to bits at being asked to do a job that he said: 'Yes!' with a big leap. 'Yes! I will go,' he said. 'I will, I will, I will,' he said again and again and again – and off he went.

The first son sat and stewed for a while. He didn't want to go in the garden and dig, but it bugged him, the way he'd spoken to his dad, and he felt he needed to weed out his bad attitude. Suddenly he knew what to do. He stood up and said: 'I will go into the garden today.' (*Ask the actor to echo the words.*) 'I will, I will, I will,' and off he went. He picked up a spade (*ask him to mime this out*) and began to dig. He dug, he dug and he dug some more. He dug so much that he almost began to disappear down the hole he had dug. So he stopped digging and had a breather, wiping the sweat from his brow and waving at next door's cow.

Wait a second! Hang on a moment! What on earth has happened to the other son. You know, the one who said with joy that he would go and help his dad? Let's see what he is doing.

Oh, oh . . . just look at him. Just look. He's snoring. He's snoring really loudly . . . I mean *really* loudly. He said he would help his dad but in the end he couldn't be bothered. He just rested his head and went to sleep instead.

Now here is a question for you. It's time to vote with your hands. Put your left hand up if you think the first son did what his dad wanted and put your right hand up if you think the second son did what his dad wanted. (*See what the voting is like.*)

That's right! (*Always assuming that they've voted how you expected*) It was the first son who did what his dad wanted, even though he said at first he wouldn't. It makes me think how careful we have to be in what we say we are going to do. Sometimes words alone are not what's needed. Our actions can speak louder than words. Do you dig what I mean?

Prayer Father God, thank you that you are always true to your word. You always keep your promises and always mean what you say. Please help us to do the same and to be careful about what we say and to do what we've promised. Amen.

Over to you Let us be careful what we promise and make sure that we do try to keep our word.

Suggested songs *One more step*
Make me a channel of your peace
I will bring to you

Forgive what?

Where in the Bible?
Matthew 18:23-34

Way in | Have you ever done anything wrong or naughty? (*Put your own hand up to acknowledge that you have, too.*) What do we need to say when that happens?

Setting the scene | We are going to be looking at a lesson that Jesus wanted everyone to learn about saying sorry and how important it is that we forgive people. (*Choose someone to play the king and a couple of servants.*)

Story | Once there was a king. He was a good king, a wise king, a kind king, and one who liked to wave at his people – and the people liked to wave back at him. He loved them and they loved him. It was all very lovely and everybody was very happy. Well everybody apart from one of the king's servants. He was very sad.

Just look at what a sad face he has. Now that *is* sad. He was so sad he cried. Really loudly. That's right. He was very sad, miserable and full of woes, saying things like: 'Oh my, oh my, I'm full of woes.'

He felt so blue – so down in the dumps – because he owed the king some money. Not just a penny or a pound but a whole bucket of money, and what did he have to pay back the king? Did he have a bucket full of money? Did he have a pound or a penny? No. He didn't have any. So what was he to do? What was the king going to do when he faced him one day and told him the truth?

The servant fell on his knees and begged the king:

'Pretty please, pretty please,
    I don't have any money,
    I'm not being funny,
    I have an awful queasy tummy
    and I want my mummy!'

The king looked at the sad, sorrowful face and felt full of compassion and grace.

'I forgive you every penny. Don't cry, go and tell your mummy.'

So the servant thanked the king and jumped for joy, then set off for home with a bone to pick. Or should I say a fellow servant to pick on.

'Oi, you!' he shouted in the street,
    as he saw a servant starting to retreat.
    'You owe me a shiny penny,
    now pay up if you have any.'

Oh dear, oh dear, oh dear, the servant didn't have one single penny, so he fell to his knees begging his fellow servant: 'Please, pretty please, can you forgive me? I'll give you my last bit of cheese.'

'Cheese!' thundered the other servant.

> 'Cheese! I don't want your cheese,
>   you snivelling servant,
>   grovelling on your knees,
>   now that you've failed
>   you're going to be *jailed*'

And that's what he did. He threw the poor man in jail because he couldn't pay back the penny. Even though he'd been forgiven so much he quickly forgot and he didn't pass on the generosity of the king. Ah, the king. What would he do when he got to hear?

When the king heard he decided to have a word in the ear of his servant and said:

> 'I forgave you a lot of money
>   and I don't find your actions very funny.
>   You should have forgiven too
>   instead of making me feel blue.
>   Now you've made a wrong decision
>   it's off you go to prison!'

The king banished the man to jail and released the other servant, who was very very pleased and politely said: 'Thank you.'

Prayer Father God, thank you that you forgive us when we say sorry and mean it. Please help us to be like you and to forgive. Amen.

Over to you Why is forgiveness so important? Remember that the cross is all about how much God forgave us, and in the Lord's Prayer Jesus teaches us to forgive one another, too.

Suggested songs *I'm accepted, I'm forgiven*
Make me a channel of your peace
Give me joy in my heart

Anyone for a party?

Where in the Bible?
Matthew 22:1-10

Way in | Do you like going to parties? How do you feel when you receive an invitation to a party?

Setting the scene | We are going to be looking at a story Jesus told that was all about people being invited to a party. (*Ask for some volunteers. You will need a king, a servant and a messenger.*)

Story | This is the story all about a king – a kind king, a good king, a friendly king and a wise king. He cared about his people and he loved them all very much. He loved them so much that he decided to throw a really big party. Imagine the biggest party that you can. Well, it was going to be bigger than that. Imagine the biggest bouncy castle you can. Well, there was going to be a bouncy castle as big as the king's castle. It was going to be that kind of party. So the king sent out his messenger to deliver the invitations. (*Select a few more people.*)

When the messenger arrived back at the palace the king wanted to know how successful they'd been and if people were coming to the party. They had a little chat and then they waited. They waited . . . and they waited . . . and they waited (*whistle nervously, drum fingers on a table*). Then they waited some more, and after they had finished waiting they waited again. No one was coming – no one at all. There was only one thing to do. They would send out the messenger to find out if they were coming. The royal messenger raced out of the palace and into the city to find out if the people were coming to the party.

At the first house the person opened the door and said: 'No, I'm staying in to watch the telly.' At the next house the person said they were staying in to watch the paint dry. It was a lovely colour and they didn't want to miss it. At the last house – the very last house – the person just shouted through the letterbox: 'No.' The messenger tried to ask them nicely. 'Are you coming to the party?' he said. But the person simply shouted: 'No!', and no matter how many times he asked, the person just kept on shouting: 'No, No, No!'

Oh dear, oh dear, oh dear. When the servant returned to the palace he felt like a party pooper rather than a party popper. The king was very sad that nobody had responded to his invitations, but he wasn't going to give up. He sent his servant out once again, but this time he sent him far and wide, to every country lane, to the highways and the byways of the whole country. And this time, this time as the invitations were given out, the people came, one by one by one. (*You will need to orchestrate this activity.*)

When they came to the palace one by one by one, everyone –

every single one – made the king very very happy. They made him so happy he was glad he was going to have a party.

Prayer Father God, thank you that you invite everyone to come into your kingdom. Thank you for loving every one of us and inviting us to know and love you. Amen.

Over to you How can we include people? Do we keep people on the outside of our circle of friends or are we good at letting people in? Jesus loves and cares for all. His kingdom is for everyone who wants to be a part of it.

Suggested songs *Jesus' love is very wonderful*
My God is so big
O Lord, my God

What a waste

Where in the Bible?
Matthew 25:14-30

Way in | How do you feel when someone gives you some pocket money that you weren't expecting? It's exciting, isn't it? Do you think about what you might do with it?

Setting the scene | We're going to be looking at a story that Jesus told about people who had been given some money, and what they did with it. (*Ask for some volunteers. You will need a landowner and three servants.*)

Story | Once there was a landowner who owned acres and acres of land. You could stand on your tiptoe and still not see where his land ended. You could bounce up and down and still not see where his land ended.

One day he called all his servants together and told them that he was going to go on a long journey – but before he left he was going to give them some silver pieces of money, called minas. They would have to look after their minas and put them to good use. When he had given them the money he waved goodbye and set off on his journey.

The first servant had been given ten minas and he went and bought a business. She bought loads of cows, because she thought this would bring in more money. The second person decided to go to the bank and put her five minas in the highest interest account possible, so the money would grow. It was like planting seed in the ground and waiting for it to grow. But – oh dear – the third servant had a similar idea, but he got it wrong. He was so worried about losing the money, so scared of wasting it, so frightened of failing, that he dug a big hole in the ground and then when the hole was huge he plopped his mina inside and covered it up with dirt again. He was very relieved and very happy.

Days passed, weeks flew by, months sailed by and the years came and went with no sign of the return of the landowner – until one day, they could see him in the distance, walking towards the house. They were all pleased to see him and waved happily. He waved back. It was a happy reunion, and before long he wanted to know what they had done with the money he had given them.

The first servant showed him a field of cows and a booming business. The second servant showed him a bank statement which showed how the money had grown. The third servant pointed to a hole in the ground.

A hole in the ground!

The landowner couldn't believe what he was hearing.

A hole in the ground?

A hole in the ground!

Yes, a hole in the ground. The servant dug down and brought out the one single, not so shiny, coin, and handed it back.

The landowner wasn't very pleased. The servant had wasted his money and acted very foolishly, so he took away his one coin and gave it to the one who'd made the most. He sent the man away to learn some common sense.

Prayer Father God, thank you for the gifts and talents that you have given us. Please help us not to lose them or misuse them but to use them properly. Amen.

Over to you How do we use our gifts and talents? What would happen if we just ignored or buried our gifts? Why do you think people might decide to use them? How about us?

Suggested songs *If I were a butterfly*
I give my hands
I, the Lord of sea and sky

The whining workers

Where in the Bible?
Matthew 20:1-15

Way in | Does anyone like receiving rewards? How does it make you feel?

Setting the scene | This story is based on a parable that Jesus told about the kingdom of heaven. (*Ask for some volunteer actors. You will need four to start with.*)

Story | This story is all about a man – a man who owned a farm. He had plenty of animals to look after and he was very good at imitating their voices. (*Ask the volunteers to do a few impressions – i.e a cow, a duck, a pig and a crocodile!*) He also had acres and acres of land. So much land that it took him ages to look after everything. In fact, he needed some helpers, some other workers. So, early in the morning, just as the sun was rising, he set out to hire some people.

The first person he found was only half awake.

'Hello! Would you like a job? I'll pay you £50 for the day.'

'£50!' said the man who was suddenly wide awake. '£50! When can I start?' So off to work he went with a shovel and a pick, singing a little song called 'Hi-ho'. (*Sing 'Hi-ho, hi-ho, it's off to work I go,' and get the children to join in.*)

The man found someone else who was half asleep and said: 'Would you like some work? I'll pay you £50.'

'£50!' the person said, now wide awake. 'When can I start?' and off to work they went. (*Hi-ho . . .*)

The man needed more workers so a few hours later he found someone who was looking very bored. Really bored and really sad.

'Why are you sad?' he asked.

'Because I don't have a job and nobody will hire me,' he cried.

'I will,' said the man and he set him to work.

In the late afternoon the man realised he still needed more workers so he looked for someone he could hire. 'Yes, you,' he said.

And out came another worker. But at the end of the day, with just one hour to go, he still needed someone else, so he looked and he saw another worker and he said: 'Yes you,' and out she came.

At the end of the day all the workers lined up in a nice straight line ready to be paid.

The worker who was hired last received . . . £50! Yes, £50. She couldn't believe it.

'I can't believe it!'

The men on the end of the line said: 'We can't believe it.'

They also started to rub their hands together, thinking how much they would get.

'£50,' said the man. 'Just as we agreed.'

'£50! £50?' they repeated, and they started to moan and groan.

'£50,' said the man. 'Just as we agreed.'

But the workers were still moaning and groaning.

'We've done more work than them,' they complained.

The man looked at them all and said: 'Friend, I am not being unfair to you. Didn't you agree to work for £50? Take your pay and go. I want to give the person who was hired last the same as I gave you. Don't I have the right to do what I want with my own money? Or are you envious because I am generous?'

Prayer Father God, thank you that you are generous and give us what we don't deserve and could never earn. Thank you for your grace. Amen.

Over to you Why do you think the workers reacted like they did? Why is it good to be generous? How can we be generous in our lives? Grace is God's love and generosity to us. We cannot earn or deserve it but we can receive it.

Suggested songs *Give me joy in my heart*
Come on and celebrate
Rejoice in the Lord always

Solid as a sandcastle

Where in the Bible?
Matthew 7:24-27

Way in	Are you good at listening and doing? It's hard sometimes, because it's not just a case of hearing the words of our teachers or families but actually putting them into practice.
Setting the scene	Jesus told a story all about the need to listen carefully and act wisely.
Scene	There are two narrators on stage, at stage right and left. In the centre stage are two actors, Mr or Mrs Sandcastle and Mr or Mrs Practice. (*They're written as Mr in the script, so just adapt as necessary.*)
Narrator 1	This is a story about two people.
Narrator 2	Which is why there are two people waving at you now. (*The two narrators glare at the two actors. One of them, Mr Practice, is waving; the other one, Mr Sandcastle, is stroking his chin and looking around the room, daydreaming.*)
N1	Ahem! This is a story about two people.
N2	Which is why there are *two*, I said *two* people waving now. Ahem! 'Now!' (*Mr Sandcastle finally gets the message and begins to wave, quite frantically.*)
N1	Mr Practice was a very good builder . . .
Mr Practice	I'm a very good builder.
N2	Mr Sandcastle was also a very good builder . . .
Mr Sandcastle	I'm also a very good builder.
N1	When they went to school they liked to build things.
Mr P	When I went to school I liked to build things.
Mr S	When I was at school I liked to build things, too.
N1	When they got older they liked to build houses . . .
N2	Big houses.
Mr P	Now that we're older we like to build houses . . .
Mr S	Big houses.
N1	Mr Practice employed all kinds of people. He employed architects. (*On walks someone carrying a pen and a pad. Stands next to Mr Practice and looks very serious, scribbling things in their pad.*) He employed builders. (*On walk a few people who flex their muscles to show that they are strong. They then mime out a simple building action that is done repetitively during this part of the sketch.*) And he employed a surveyor (*enter a surveyor, who stands on his tiptoes and looks around him with his hand to his eyes in an exaggerated way*).
Surveyor	I can't see anything on the horizon, what am I meant to be looking at?
N1	You're not surveying the land – you're surveying the house and the ground.
Surveyor	Oh, sorry, silly me. (*He goes and stands by the architect and looks at the plans, nodding his head as he does so.*)

N2	Mr Sandcastle employed a deckchair attendant. (*All the other characters with Mr Practice stop what they are doing and look across at Mr Sandcastle and together they say: 'A what?'*)
N2	I said Mr Sandcastle employed a deckchair attendant. (*Mr Sandcastle smiles and looks pleased with himself. On walks someone with a deckchair. Mr Sandcastle looks really pleased and sits down in it.*)
N2	He employed someone to bring him a pair of sunglasses. (*All the other characters say: 'A pair of what?'*)
N2	I said he employed someone to bring him a pair of sunglasses. (*On walks someone with a pair of sunglasses, who puts them on Mr Sandcastle.*)
N2	And he employed someone to bring him a bucket and spade. (*All the characters say: 'A what?'*)
N2	I said he employed someone to bring him a bucket and spade. (*Someone walks on carrying a bucket and spade, which they give to Mr Sandcastle, who looks very pleased with them.*)
N2	Because Mr Sandcastle built his house on the . . .
Mr S	. . . Sand! (*He jumps up now*) Yes, the sand . . . because I do love building sandcastles. (*All the other characters shake their heads.*)
N1	That's very nice, but what about when it . . .
Mr P	Rains (*he looks up and they all mime it raining – they could hold out their palms and pretend that they are catching raindrops, then they all go inside Mr Practice's house and shut the door*).
N1	The rain fell and the storm blew, but the house was built on solid rock, and nothing could get through.
N2	Oh dear, oh dear, oh dear, oh dear.
Mr S	What? What?
N2	Mr Sandcastle, look at your house.
Mr S	What house? (*He looks and sees that his house is sinking.*)
Mr S	Ah! My house is sinking. I have a sinking feeling about how this story is going to end. (*He hides behind his deckchair.*)
N1	Mr Practice always put wise words into practice and built his house on a solid foundation.
N2	But Mr Sandcastle built his house on sand because he didn't put into practice what was sensible and right – and so his house fell with a great crash. (*The deckchair is crashed on the floor and Mr Sandcastle cries. All the people in Mr Practice's house pull out a tissue and hold it out for him.*)
Prayer	Father God, thank you that you do speak to us through the Bible. Please help us to be wise in the way we build our lives. Amen.
Over to you	Why did the man's house crash? What could he have done differently? Why is building on a solid foundation so important? What we listen to and what we believe will affect the way we live. Let's be careful in what we do believe and what we do practise.
Suggested songs	*Don't build your house on the sandy land* *He's got the whole world in his hand* *I give my hands to do your work*

Some kind of friend

Where in the Bible?
Luke 11:5-8

Way in	What are you like at asking for things? Do you pester your mums and dads? Do you ask lots of questions in class? It is good to ask for help because we all need it. Sometimes it can be awkward asking for help if people are very busy or tired.
Setting the scene	We're looking at a story that Jesus told all about prayer and we're going to finish by asking God to help us.
Scene	There are two narrators on stage at either side. In the middle there is a boy and a girl who are both asleep, and a short distance away from them are two boys and two girls who are asleep.
Narrator 1	This is a bedtime story.
Narrator 2	So, as you can see, everyone is sound asleep before we even speak. (*All the characters do some snoring.*)
N1	But the story starts when one family start to wake up because there is a . . .
N2	. . . knock on the door.
N1	Knock, knock.
N2	No one stirs, no one wakes up, so there is a louder . . .
N1	Knock! Knock!
N2	Which wakes the man and his wife up. (*They both jump, rub their eyes and look around them.*)
Man	There's someone at the door.
Wife	Well, you'd better go and open it then. I have to have my beauty sleep.
M	Yes you do.
W	Pardon? What are you insinuating?
M	Nothing, dear, I'm going to the door.
N1	He quickly went to the door and found . . .
M	(*He pretends to open the door.*) There's no one there. (*He looks confused.*)
N2	Wait a second; I'm not there yet. (*Narrator 2 hurries across and now acts out the part of the friend at midnight.*)
M	Oh, it's you!
N1	It was an old old friend whom he hadn't seen since . . .
M	Playtime.
N1	(*Narrator 1 glares at him.*) Since they were at school together.
M	We still are at school (*looking confused.*)
N1	(*Narrator 1 walks over to explain.*) I know we are still at school, but we are acting, remember, this is a sketch, OK?
M	OK. Sorry. (*Narrator 1 walks back.*)

49

M	I haven't seen you since we were at school together. Come in. (*They step inside the house.*)
N2	I've travelled a long way and it's good to be here, but I'm really hungry, so can you give me some food, please? (*Man looks shocked.*)
M	Back in a mo. (*He dashes to his wife, wakes her up. She is not very happy*)
W	What on earth is going on?
N1	So he quickly explained (*He acts out explaining*), and his wife was shocked (*she acts shocked*) because tomorrow was their supermarket shopping day, so they didn't have any food in the house. (*The man goes back to his friend.*)
M	I won't be long. I'm just popping out to feed the, er, goldfish. I won't be long.
N1	So out he went . . . (*The friend has now turned back into the narrator*)
N2	. . . Across the road to his neighbour's house.
N1	Where everyone was sound asleep. (*They all start to snore loudly*)
N2	The man knocked on the door . . .
M	Knock, knock.
N1	He knocked even louder . . .
M	Knock! Knock!
N2	But still no one came.
N1	So he started to shout . . .
M	Shout, shout.
N2	And shout louder still . . .
M	Shout! Shout!
N1	Until the family woke up. (*They all wake up and look very grumpy. The man goes to the door.*)
Man 2	Hey, what do you think you're doing. We were all asleep!
N2	The man tried to explain.
N1	He was sorry for being a pain.
N2	But he needed to borrow something to eat.
N1	Then he would clear off up the street.
N2	The neighbour wasn't very happy.
N1	But gave some food to the chappy.
N2	Who became happy and clappy (*starts to act happy and clap*).
N1	And went home with a skip. (*He skips back to his house.*)
N2	And had some food for his friend, who'd made the long trip.
M	(*Acts out giving food to N2.*)
N1	And this is the end of our bedtime story, so it's time we all went to . . . (*They all close their eyes and snore.*)
Prayer	Father God, thank you that you welcome us when we call out to you. Thank you that you do hear our prayers and respond to our requests. Amen.
Over to you	Jesus told this parable to encourage us to talk to God and be bold enough to ask him to help us. No matter who we are or how good we feel, God loves us and wants to hear from us. He can help us if we ask him.
Suggested songs	*My God is so big*

The light of understanding

Where in the Bible?
Matthew 5:14-16

Way in	What would you think if you gave someone a gift and they put it in a cupboard and never used it! The talents we have are a gift from God, and that's what this morning's assembly is about.
Setting the scene	We're going to look at some teaching that Jesus gave about not hiding our lights – our gifts and our talents – but letting them shine.
Scene	There are two narrators at either side of the stage and two actors who are also on opposite sides. They have their backs to each other.
Narrator 1	This is the story of two people.
Narrator 2	Who are very friendly people.
N1	They would wave to you and say . . .
N2	. . . Hello!
N1	If they could see you.
N2	But they can't.
N1	Because it is dark.
N2	It is night time.
N1	It is pitch black.
N2	And our friends are about to realise that they are not . . .
N1	Alone! (*The two actors start to walk slowly into the centre of the stage. They are still back to back and as they progress it is obvious what is going to happen – they are going to bump into each other.*)
N2	If we were not narrating the story . . .
N1	But were a part of the story . . .
N2	Then we would shout . . .
N1/N2	Watch out!
N2	But, alas we are mere narrators of the text . . .
N1	Back to back, our friends bump into each other. (*They bump into each other and jump up.*)
Beryl	Ouch!
Andy	Ow!
B	Who is that?
A	Who's there? (*They stand almost next to each other but unable to see, both peering into the darkness.*)
B	You answer me, I asked first.
A	Yeah, but I spoke loudest.
B	Is that Andy?
A	Yeah, is that Beryl?
B	Yeah.
A	Nice to see you. (*He holds out his hand to shake hands, and so does Beryl, but their hands miss one another. They shake thin air instead.*)

B	Andy?
A	Yeah.
B	Don't you have a torch?
A	Yes.
B	Didn't you bring it with you?
A	Yes (*he leans forward to whisper*) it's in my pocket.
N1	On hearing this information Beryl gasps.
B	Gasp!
N2	She finds this information hard to believe.
B	I find this information hard to believe.
N1	Why is Andy's torch in his pocket?
B	Andy, why is your torch in your pocket?
N2	Why isn't he using it?
B	Why aren't you using it?
A	(*Smiles, knowingly.*) I'm saving the batteries.
B	You're saving the batteries! You're saving the batteries!
A	That's what I said.
N1	'Why is he saving his batteries on a dark and windy night?' Beryl wondered.
B	Why are you saving your batteries on a dark and windy night, I wonder. (*When she says the words 'windy night' both Beryl and Andy start to sway from side to side.*)
N2	'Why not use the torch on a dark, windy, rainy night?' Beryl wondered.
B	Why not use the torch on a dark, windy and rainy night, I wonder. (*Both actors start to act out as if it is suddenly raining.*)
A	I don't want to get my torch wet, do I?
B	But it's dark.
A	I know.
B	And windy.
A	I know.
B	And raining.
A	I know.
B	So use your torch!
N1	What will happen next in our exciting saga?
N2	Tune in next week to find out. (*They all freeze for a moment then Beryl turns to the narrators.*)
B	But we're not doing the assembly next week.
A	I'm getting wet. Can we stop now?
Prayer	Father God, thank you for showing us how to live life. Please help us not to hide away our talents but to use them and help one another. Amen.
Over to you	What would happen if we didn't use our gifts and talents? Who would miss out? How can we let our light shine?
Suggested songs	*This little light of mine* *Give me oil in my lamp* *Lord, the light of your love*

Running the race

Where in the Bible?
Luke 8:1-15

Way in | What are you like at persevering? Do you give up and give in when the going gets tough or do you keep on going? Thumbs up, thumbs down and thumbs in the middle – let's see what you're like. Sometimes we are good at keeping on going and other times we are not. (*You may want to share a personal story to highlight this.*)

Setting the scene | We are going to hear a story that Jesus told based on the parable of the sower.

Scene | Four athletes warming up on the track. After a few stretches they take up their starting positions.

Commentator | The athletes are poised on the track, ladies and gentlemen. The race of their life is about to begin. Awaiting starter's orders. (*In a disguised voice.*) On your marks, get set . . . go!

(*Three of the runners come out of their starting blocks and begin the race – this is done in slow motion. One of the runners remains in the starting blocks – a position they remain in for the rest of the sketch.*)

Oh dear, I don't think one of the runners understands that the race has begun! No, I'm afraid they don't. Just look at that puzzled expression.

(*The runner who hasn't started the race is looking round in a very dazed way.*)

Let's see how the race is progressing. Looks like we have an early leader.

(*One of the runners is a few steps in front of the others. He looks back and grins. Suddenly the smile disappears from his face, he stops pumping his arms and grabs hold of his legs.*)

It looks like he's in some difficulty. He could still carry on . . .

(*The runner shakes his head.*)

. . . or he could give up . . .

(*The runner nods his head and hobbles off the track.*)

Now there are only two competitors left in the race. Whoever wins this race is going to be world famous overnight. They will appear on all the sports pages, they will be asked for countless interviews, they will have to deal with intense media pressures, they will find their life is never the same again!

(*While this is being said one of the runners looks very worried, pulls anxious faces, bites their fingernails until eventually, their mind full of worries, they stop running and walk away.*)

Oh dear, was it something I said? There is now only one runner left in the race. He is bound to win if he keeps on running to the end. The finishing line is in sight. He must be in a lot of pain, but will he keep going? He's nearly crossed the line, the tape is in sight, and . . .

(*The runner crosses the line, holds his arms aloft, freezes in victory position.*)

. . . Yes! The race is won!

Prayer

Father God, thank you that you never give up on us. Please help us to be more like you, we pray. Amen.

Over to you

Relate how the sketch is similar to the parable of the sower. If we don't listen or understand the message we will never get out of the starter's blocks. We will lose our way if we become distracted or worried about things. Only when we hear and understand the message and keep on putting it into practice will we bear much fruit for our labours.

Suggested songs

I will bring to you
Make me a channel of your peace
One more step along the world

The parable of Pru

Where in the Bible?
Luke 15:8-10

Way in	Have you ever lost anything? How did you feel? (*You may want to give a personal example from your own life.*)
Setting the scene	Today's story is based on a parable that Jesus taught. (*There are two narrators on stage and Pru. Narrator 2 is standing still and there is a coin under their foot.*)
Narrator 1	This is the story about Pru.
Pru	Hello, I'm Pru.
Narrator 2	Pru was always very careful what to do.
P	I'm always careful what to do.
N1	She would look after her house.
N2	Making it look so clean and nice.
N1	Making sure there were no scurrying mice.
P	I make sure there are no scurrying mice.
N2	One thing that Pru loved above all the rest.
N1	One thing that Pru thought was the best.
N2	Were her precious, shiny coins that she kept locked away.
N1	She would look at them and count them once each day.
P	Oh it's my favourite time of day now. Time to count my precious coins. (*Pru goes and picks up a little box. She opens it and looks inside.*)
P	I wonder if you can guess how many coins I have inside? (*She invites the children to guess.*)
P	Ten. Ten is the answer. Ten precious, shiny coins. Now it's time for me to count them all. One, two, three, four, five, six, seven, eight, nine . . . nine?! (*Pru looks shocked when she realises.*)
P	I think I'd better count them again. One . . . two . . . three . . . four . . . five . . . six . . . seven . . . eight . . . nine . . .! Oh no, one of my coins is missing. Whatever am I going to do?
N2	Pru was very upset.
N1	She didn't know what to do. (*As they say the next lines Pru acts out what they are saying.*)
N2	She looked on the stairs.
N1	And under them, too.
N2	She swept all the floors.
N1	And above all the doors.
N2	But Pru couldn't find her coin.
N1	What was she to do?
P	I know! I'll get out my lamp. I'll shine it in every corner of my house. I'm sure I can find it soon, I hope!
N2	So Pru lit a lamp and began to look.

N1	On top of the piano and inside a book.
N2	She looked high, she looked low.
N1	Until there was nowhere left to go.
P	Oh no! Now what can I do? I think I need some help. *(Ask for a volunteer to come and help. Ask them to look in one direction, to where Narrator 2 is standing.)*
N1	With help from her neighbour.
N2	Pru looked some more.
N1	Until her good friend.
N2	Found the coin on the floor. *(Narrator 2 lifts their foot to reveal the coin to the volunteer.)*
P	Oh, thank you so much. I am so happy I could throw a party. Why not? I'll invite all the neighbours, but first I think I'll put my coin safely away.

Prayer	Father God, thank you that you care about us and that every one of us is special and precious to you. Amen.
Over to you	Ask the children why they thought the lady in the story kept on looking for her coin and didn't give up until she found it. Ask what that teaches us about God.
Suggested songs	*This is the day* *O Lord, my God* *He's got the whole world in his hands*